W9-BNS-244
Kent WA

Street Skateboarding:
Endless Grinds and Slides

Street Skateboarding: Endless Grinds and Slides

Evan Goodfellow
with Doug Werner

Photography by
Tadashi Yamaoda

Tricks performed by Evan Goodfellow
and friends

Tracks Publishing
San Diego, California

Street Skateboarding:
Endless Grinds and Slides

Evan Goodfellow with Doug Werner

Tracks Publishing
140 Brightwood Avenue
Chula Vista, CA 91910
619-476-7125
tracks@cox.net
www.startupsports.com

All rights reserved. No part of this book may be reproduced or transmitted in any form or by any means, electronic or mechanical, including photocopying, recording or by any information storage and retrieval system without permission from the author, except for the inclusion of brief quotations in a review.

Copyright © 2005 by Doug Werner
10 9 8 7 6 5 4 3 2

Publisher's Cataloging-in-Publication

Goodfellow, Evan.
    Street skateboarding : endless grinds and slides /
Evan Goodfellow with Doug Werner ; photography by
Tadashi Yamaoda ; tricks performed by Evan Goodfellow
and friends.
    p. cm.
    Includes index.
    LCCN 2005900868
    ISBN 1-884654-23-1

    1. Skateboarding.   I. Werner, Doug, 1950-
II. Title.

GV859.8.G66 2005   796.22
                           QBI05-200030

I dedicate this book to
my friends and family.
Thanks for everything.

Acknowledgements

Thanks to

Tadashi Yamaoda
for finding spots and riders, performing tricks and taking photos

Dave Coyne,
Cody Branin
and **Gilbert Martin**
for performing tricks.

Jim Montalbano
for graphic production

Phyllis Carter
for editing with her mighty red pen

www.metrofoundation.net
clothing and apparel

Preface

Skateboarding can be a wonderful as well as a frustrating experience, especially for riders who want to progress and learn new tricks. Most skateboarders learn through trial and error and figure out tricks on their own. The purpose of this book is to help individuals learn and understand how curb tricks are performed. Although curb tricks constitute only one aspect of skateboarding, they provide a base for so many other tricks.

Curb tricks are a great challenge for skateboarders. Grinds and slides can be mastered on obstacles found in almost every city or town. Skateboarders can wax a curb near their home instead of having to build a ramp or box. The only cost is a piece of wax. Learn tricks on curbs and take those same tricks to ramps and rails. That's progression. Taking on the continual challenge is what makes skateboarding great.

The photographer and I took on the challenge of writing this book. We combined words and pictures to explain how to perform specific tricks. Pictures speak volumes regarding positioning and physical motion. The words help readers better understand the pictures and explain the thought processes required to perform each trick. This was a difficult task and we hope the captions and pictures are suitable guides. We want readers to have fun as they learn.

Because skateboarding is all about having fun and enjoying a culture that is truly distinctive. I hope this book encourages readers to further their fun and ability in the sport we all love so much.

Evan Goodfellow

Warning label

Skateboarding can be dangerous. Riders should know and follow safe skateboarding procedures and wear appropriate safety gear at all times. Although riders in this book do not wear safety gear, we do not endorse riding without it.

Contents

Skating technique and style initially took cues from surfing.

Intro

Welcome to the world of street skateboarding. The main purpose of this book is to teach the reader how to do a vast assortment of curb tricks. These tricks lay the foundation for true core street skating.

Early days, early terrain

Skateboarding has come a long way since its early days when kids strapped roller skate wheels to a piece of wood and cruised the streets. Skating's first boom hit in the early '60s. It took some time before we knew if the sport would continue to advance or whether it would fizzle out. Other midcentury fads like the pogo stick or Hula-Hoop provided instant amusement but did not become true sports with lasting followings. Skating, however, survived various ups and downs over the years and has become a major pursuit, sport and lifestyle. Top skaters compete for big prize money and appear in movies, commercials, video games, books and magazines. There are millions of skaters worldwide and millions of wannabes or posers simply dressing up to look like them.

Skating technique and style initially took cues from surfing. Individuals like Tony Alva and members of the legendary Dog Town team took concepts of cruising and carving to the streets and ultimately into drained swimming pools of Southern California. In the pools riders dealt with the curvature of the cement and began to develop transitional skating — that is, skating

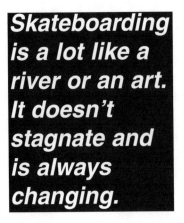

Skateboarding is a lot like a river or an art. It doesn't stagnate and is always changing.

from a flat level to an incline.

Technique and equipment continued to evolve. Skaters built wood ramps to experiment further with transitional skating. Wood ramps called half pipes were created to provide terrain similar to cement pools. Instead of cement tops or coping, metal or plastic piping was put on top of the half pipes for riders to grind or slide.

Half pipe construction was an event that created friendships and provided endless hours of fun. Skateboarders gathered together to contribute wood and time to build half pipes in friends' back yards or out in the countryside. Willing parents soon discovered that word in the skateboard community spread quickly. When a half pipe went up in a neighborhood, that back yard became the local hangout. Individuals who could not afford to build half pipes built smaller launch ramps.

Jump ramps provided a means to launch ever farther and get more air. Tricks such as grabs and different grab variations were invented. These ramps were practical because they could be carried or dragged out by one or two people. In the early to mid-'80s you would see the coolest skaters with a launch in the back of their truck. After school or on weekends, they would pull out the ramp on a side street or parking lot and the kids would gather.

Street skating

Skateboarding is a lot like a river or an art. It doesn't
stagnate and is always changing. Once something
becomes mastered or tiresome, skaters change direc-
tion, create new challenges and seek new avenues. Just
as carving became old news, so did half pipes and
pools. Then along came street skating. Street skating uti-
lizes the objects and obstacles commonly found in
urban areas. Sliding and grinding concrete objects is
not easy. That's why wax comes in handy. Skaters the
world over found that applying the right amount of
wax to most any curb created a suitable skating surface. Painted curbs are great to skate as is. The paint
creates a smooth, slippery surface that boards can slide
or grind across easily.

This change of environments created hard times for
many skateboarders who had made a career and small
fortunes from sponsorships based on half pipe and
pool skating. Mark Ragowlski was a skateboard hero
whose career was damaged because he could not make
the transition to street skating.

Skateboarders who excelled on street terrain included
Matt Hensley, Mark Gonzales, Mike Valley and Tom
Knox. They did their grinds and sliding on benches,
curbs or anything found on everyday streets. In an early
H-Street video, Matt Hensley had a part during the
song, "Going to the Store with Matt Hensley." It featured
Mr. Hensley going to the store and doing tricks along
the way.

The types of tricks done on curbs were similar and
identical in some instances to tricks learned on half

> *Skateboarders are unique. They have always stood out from the football players, basketball players and other athletes.*

pipes. Many required an individual simply to turn on to the curb, while others involved the ollie, which is the trick that causes all four wheels to come off the ground. The favorite tricks of the early curb days were rail slides and 50-50 grinds.

Just as the terrain of choice was changing to meet the growing interest of skateboarders, so was the equipment. Skateboard companies raced to keep up with the change of environment creating skateboards and board parts that performed better. Boards soon had plastic rail guards, skid plates on the tail and plastic nose guards. Plastic rails provided the capability to slide across a curb without the need for wax.

Santa Cruz Skateboards created a layer called Ever Slick, which resulted in a lighter board that outperformed plastic rails. It was said that wax was no longer needed and that Ever Slicks were the new technology of skateboarding.

Skateboarding culture

You come across the word culture growing up. Teachers discuss culture with you early, and as you travel or come in contact with people from other parts of the country or world, you begin to know and understand what the word means. Culture describes the features or characteristics of a group of people that make them unique. I am from Canada and moved to California when I was 20. Californians pointed out the things that were unique to my Canadian culture. The fact that I would say "eh" after a sentence or the way I pronounced "about" more like "aboot."

One of the big draws of skateboarding is its culture. Skateboarders are unique. They have always stood out from the football players, basketball players and other athletes. Skateboarding culture was built on the image of the rebel or nonconformist. In the early days this culture was defined by the music skaters listened to, the way they dressed and the overall feeling of being different and separate from everyone else. Skateboarders even had haircuts that were unique called skater cuts.

I attended a rough elementary public school. In first grade I remember walking by the principal's office and seeing big stacks of skateboards confiscated from the older students' lockers. Skateboards were not allowed, but there was a group who chose to rebel by bringing them anyway. The clothes they wore and their style of hair or hats made these individuals stand out. Their shirts often bore the Vision Street Wear logo, which represented the culture of young people who spent their time in the street skating.

I wanted to be like them. I talked about skateboarding with my parents. One of my first-grade classmates had brothers in that older, rebel group. His parents bought him a board and skate clothes so he could ride with his brothers. He soon became the coolest kid on the planet to me. I took note of what he wore and what kind of

> *Skateboarding draws on its history and continues to attract individuals who don't fit the suburban kid mold — a paper route and hopes of getting into a good college.*

board he had. I could only dream of the day when I had my own board.

I was in the fourth grade when I was able to afford a pro board. I choose a Powell Steve Caballero. The board had a dragon on the bottom, and the guy at the skate shop told me it was one of the best. I remember skating to school when my friend from the first grade made fun of me for wanting to be a skater. He called me a poser. Then his older brother took a look at my new board and asked if he could try it. He did an ollie and said that it was cool that I wanted to start skating. He hit his little brother and called him a dork for making fun of me. That was my initiation into the skateboarding community.

There seems to be more acceptance for skateboarders than there used to be. Today at schools you see individuals who don't skate wearing skate shoes or skateboard clothing. Skate style is mainstream. In the early days of skateboarding there was much more separation and distinction between those who skated and those who did not. Those who only wore the clothing were labeled as posers meaning someone who was wanting to look like a skater but could not actually skate. The popularity of skateboarding has helped get the sport recognized, but it has also robbed it of its uniqueness.

Recently a pro skateboarder talked about the uniqueness of the skateboarding culture in an interview. He said that the draw for him and many others to skateboarding is that skateboarders are so cool. The classic cultural image of skateboarding is similar to the image one thinks of when you see a tatooed dude riding a Harley Davidson wearing a leather jacket looking tough as hell. The rough, tough image is something that drew and attracted me, too. But the image of skateboarding has mellowed.

Although posers abound, those that stick with the sport seem to be as true as the skaters in the early days. Skateboarding draws on its history and continues to attract individuals who don't fit the suburban kid mold — a paper route and hopes of getting into a good college. Skateboarding has drawn individuals from broken homes or those who are independent. The sport fosters independence because there is no coach, and there is no real support to be an Olympic skateboarder. The reason why individuals stay with it is because they truly enjoy it.

Skateboarding will always maintain its unique culture that bonds all skaters. You can travel anywhere on earth and find skateboarders. Mutual passion and shared knowledge cements the international bond. Skaters talk about recent skate magazines or videos, the latest tricks, good skate spots and share a special comradeship.

> *Most people don't realize that there is an important learning curve involved. Before the pro learns the trick on the rail, he must master it on the curb. Curbs are the practicing ground for rail tricks.*

Curb tricks are foundational

Skateboard magazines and videos continually feature big tricks down handrails. These tricks become more impressive and mind blowing as the skateboarder does more complicated moves down ever greater numbers of stairs. These riders require precise technical skills and the ability to overcome fears. Most people don't realize that there is an important learning curve involved. Before the pro learns the trick on the rail, he must master it on the curb. Curbs are the practicing ground for rail tricks.

On the Zero Skateboards Web site, a survey asked what skaters would rather watch, curb tricks or rail tricks. Curb tricks topped the poll. Rail rides are very impressive to watch, but are the cause of many skateboarding injuries. *Skateboarder* magazine interviewed top pro Billy Marks and asked him how he prepared for rails. He said he usually jumps down the stairs a few times to warm up. Then he goes for it and expects to be unable to walk for several days. Rail riders do not enjoy a long skateboarding career.

Although some pros are able to do huge gaps and rails safely, most suffer from knee, ankle and back damage due to the impact from falls. Skaters do large rails in hopes of getting and keeping a sponsor. Many skateboarders will not jump down a set of stairs or go down a rail without a camera or video camera capturing the trick.

I met a talented ninth grader in California who was hoping to be sponsored by a large company. He felt he had to do the big tricks, and he got really good at handrails and gaps. He could switch ollie 11 stairs and frontside board slide 10-stair handrails. But he also fell. He doesn't skateboard anymore because his ankle has been twisted so many times.

Ronnie Craeger is a top pro who took a different tack when the pressures to ride rails got too much. Craeger was and still is exceptional at flat land and curb tricks. He is very smooth and can pop tricks high and land perfectly. His sponsors, however, insisted he perform more rail or stair tricks for their videos. Instead of caving, Craeger chose to quit the sponsor and remain true to his own track.

All this about rails is not to make them sound evil, but to explain that skateboarding should be more about fun and expression than trying to get big tricks and impress. Rail tricks certainly have their place. They showcase a skater's ability to take a trick to the next level. Being able to do technical tricks down big rails proves the skateboarder has talent and balls. This book hopefully will help you learn basic curb tricks for the fun of it and prepare those brave individuals who want

Professional skateboarding has become a sort of stuntman profession. Like so many Evil Kneivals, skate pros continually try to outdo each other and them- selves.

to take it to the next level on the rail.

Keeping skate- boarding fun

Go to any skate spot on a weekend in Los Angeles, and you will find the place littered with young kids riding in front of video cam- eras. If you ask them why they are being filmed, they say they are making "sponsor me" tapes. These are videos that display all the tricks a rider can do to impress skate companies in order to gain spon- sorships. You will see many of them jumping down huge sets of stairs or trying gnarly handrails because that's what sells skate magazines and videos, and that's where sponsors want their riders to be.

Professional skateboarding has become a sort of stunt- man profession. Like so many Evil Kneivals, skate pros continually try to outdo each other and themselves. A top pro, Billy Marks, says he prepares to die when he attacks a big rail. Pushing the limits on rails and stairs is fun to watch but puts a lot of pressure on the pro and puts many of them in the hospital.

Skateboarding for the sheer sake of enjoyment is another spectrum. In *Slap Magazine*, Josh Kalis recalled skating when he first turned pro in 1993. Skateboarding was not all about getting big tricks on tape. Videos simply captured a rider's ability to skate and have fun. He said today's skateboarding videos show crazy tricks but lack style. For example, it is not uncommon to see people putting hands down to help them ride away from a trick.

All the pressure to perform and outdo reminds me of sports like hockey or track that are based on performance. Parents and athletes make winning the whole point. Their goal is to be the best, and when that is not accomplished, individuals freak out and don't enjoy the sport. When success does come, it is not the sport they are enjoying as much as the success itself. The danger for skaters is pursuing the sport in hopes of gaining sponsors, and in that pursuit, forgetting the joy of riding.

Getting more technical

Skateboarding tricks evolve and advance in a variety of ways. Tricks are performed ever higher on different surfaces, influenced by individual styles and can be endlessly combined. The smith grind, for example, is a grind done on a curb, rail or ramp. At first, skateboarders find it difficult to simply land the trick. You must get on the grind with your weight in exactly the right place to pull it off. You can make it more complex by attempting it on higher curbs or rails or by doing a 180 out or shuvit out.

Tricks also become more complex by doing them switch or frontside or backside. Switch stance became popular in the mid to late '90s. Skateboarding was

Tricks that today's skateboarders are doing switch are harder than what most pros would have been able to do regular ten years ago.

becoming stagnant with few new tricks being created. That's when pros like Salman Agah, Mark Gonzales and Natas Kaupas began doing tricks switch stance. Switch stance means standing the opposite way that you normally would on a skateboard. It feels like you are learning how to ride a skateboard all over again. The basic tricks that these pros mastered with their regular stance were 100 times harder with a switch stance.

Tricks that today's skateboarders are doing switch are harder than what most pros would have been able to do regular ten years ago. Many skateboarders learn basic tricks switch at the same time they learn the same trick regular. Some riders find doing certain tricks switch easier. For example, it may be easier to turn a certain way switch because you land riding regular.

Future of skate parks

The city where I grew up had an awesome parking lot downtown at the Toys "R" Us. The curbs were different sizes and would grind really well when waxed. There was also a wide assortment of manual pads and the ground was perfect. Such a spot was impossible to find in our neighborhood. My friends and I would scrounge money to catch the bus or bum rides off people to get downtown. The one problem was that the parking lot was guarded by a security guard named Trevor. He was known to drive by at 1:00 a.m. just to see if kids were skating there. It was as if he lived to bust skateboarders.

Trevor was not a happy camper. He was about 220 pounds and kept in good shape, most likely to catch skateboarders and shoplifters. He once chased a shoplifter three blocks and beat the crap out of him before calling the police. We all knew what kind of vehicle he drove so we could run if we saw it coming. One night we were caught by surprise.

It was about 10 on a Saturday night, and there were at least a dozen of us skating. All of a sudden a strange white Bronco came ripping into the parking lot. We thought it was probably some jocks until three big guys got out and began running toward us. Someone yelled, *Trevor!* and we all knew there was going to be hell to pay. A group of us ran through the parking lot, across a busy street and headed for an alley, but Trevor was right behind. He managed to catch the whole group and began yelling at us. It turned out that the truck belonged to a friend.

Kind old Trevor decided not to press charges or call the cops. Although we felt the fear of Trevor, it did not keep us out of that parking lot. The truth is that skateboarders will do almost anything to skate a good street spot, regardless of the risk — or how good the local skate park is.

Skateboarders will do almost anything to skate a good street spot, regardless of the risk.

Skateboard videos and magazines feature street skating rather than parks. Why do cities and skateboarders keep building skate parks that are not what skaters like to skate or see on videos? Because that's the way it's always been done. City officials don't stop to think why it's more fun to skate downtown than at the skate park. This ancient lack of understanding and input from skaters on how skate parks should be built has led to trouble with city officials and police everywhere.

If you skateboard anywhere other than your driveway or local skate park, you will find out quickly that police officers, school officials and security guards do not like you skateboarding on public or private places. City officials think that the solution to keeping skateboarders off their property and other public places is to designate a spot in a local park for cement ramps and rails. When skateboarders return to the public places, officials believe they are rude and ungrateful. So what is the solution?

The solution is to make the skate park more like the street. Make curbs in the park like the curbs in front of city hall. Skateboarders want to skate "natural" spots. It's more fun to do tricks on a curb that's hard to grind and needs lots of wax than one at a skate park with a metal edge that takes no effort.

Are designated skate spots a good idea at all or do skateboarders crave incessant hassling by police and the fear of being ticketed or having their skateboards confiscated? Designated skate spots are a good idea, but design changes are needed. Pro skateboarder Rob Dyrdek and DC Shoes have created a skate park in Ohio that actually looks like a spot you would find downtown. There are no cement ramps or half pipes. There are stairs, curbs and rails like you would find at a great spot in a metropolitan area. Hopefully cities and communities will check out the natural spots their local skaters frequent and build skate parks more like those.

The solution is to make the skate park more like the street.

Curb tricks

50-50 grind

Before learning this trick you must be able to ollie up a curb. The curb requires wax, especially on the top edge because metal trucks do not naturally grind along cement. The top edge of the curb is what your trucks grind on.

Frontside 50-50

Approach the curb with the front of your body facing the curb and your feet in the ollie position. Ride toward the curb at a slight angle. Your front shoulder should be closest to the curb in order to get the

correct angle. Begin your ollie about 10 inches from the curb. Ollie up and land both trucks on the edge of the curb. Such a landing will require practice. The key is aiming your ollie so that you land correctly in the intended location.

A well waxed curb is the key to grinding. Wax after learning how to land with both trucks on the curb. The momentum of your board landing on the waxed or painted curb is what causes the trucks to grind.

Most skateboarders learn tricks in stages. The first step is where to put your feet, then how to get into the curb trick or how to flip your board. Landing the flip trick or coming out of the grind is the last step. The final step for the 50-50 is coming out and riding away. When you are slowing down on your grind, slightly lift your front truck and turn your front shoulder and foot so that you grind off the curb and land riding forward or at a slight angle.

Backside 50-50

This trick is like the frontside 50-50 in that both trucks will grind across the curb at the same time. The difference is that you ride with your back facing the curb. Your ride up to the curb should be slightly angled so

that it is easier to land on the edge of the curb with
both trucks. The angle helps you to aim your ollie. The
angle of approach will cause your front shoulder to be
closest to the curb. You should be about 10 inches
away when you begin your ollie. Ollie and land with

both trucks on the curb. Once you master getting both trucks on the curb, increase the speed so you can start grinding.

11

12

15

The frontside 50-50 and backside 50-50 are essential tricks to learn because they allow you to get more technical with curb tricks, as we will soon see. Some skateboarders are more comfortable going frontside and others prefer backside. It is good to be able to do both. Once you have successfully learned 50-50s you can advance to tricks like the nollie 50-50, fakie 50-50 and kickflip 50-50.

Kickflip backside 50-50

Master kickflips and kickflipping up a curb before you
attempt this trick. Approach the curb as if you were
doing a backside 50-50. Your feet should be in the kickflip position. Come in at a slight angle so that when

you kickflip you land on the curb in grind position. Your board should be one foot from the curb when you start the trick. Kickflip and land in the 50-50 position. Kickflip the board so that it is flipping toward the edge of the curb. You will try to catch your kickflip

before it lands on the curb so that your feet can direct the board to the proper grind position. Once you are in grind position pop off like a regular backside 50-50.

11

Frontside 5-0

Frontside 5-0s are very similar to frontside 50-50s except that when you ollie on to the curb, you place all your weight to the back foot. You should ollie about six inches away from the curb. During an ollie, your board

naturally angles up. Keep it like that without straightening it out in the air. In order to keep from slipping out as you grind, remain balanced — don't lean too far back or too far forward. Your back leg should be straight or slightly bent to hold the 5-0.

Grind off the curb by using your back foot and front foot simultaneously. This trick is easier to do at the end of a curb because you grind straight off.

Backside 5-0

Approach the curb at a very slight angle. Ollie about six inches from it. Ollie as you would for a backside 50-50 and keep your board from leveling out in the air. As your back truck lands on the curb, keep all your weight

on the back foot. Keep your back leg straight or at a slight bend to hold the 5-0 position. When you are done grinding, turn off the curb by using your back foot and front foot simultaneously.

Frontside nosegrind

Approach the curb with your front facing the curb. Begin to ollie when you are about six inches from the curb. Pop an ollie and as you level off in the air, extend your front leg so that the nose of your board points

downward. As your front truck lands on the curb, keep your front leg extended and your back leg slightly bent in order to hold the grind. When you come off the curb, give the board a little push forward with your front foot so your back truck does not hit the curb.

After you give the board the push, extend your back leg so that your board levels out and you land on both sets of wheels.

Backside nosegrind

Approach the curb with your back facing the curb.
Ollie as if you are doing a backside 50-50, but while in
the air, extend your front leg so that your board lands
in the nosegrind position. Keep your balance centered

on your front leg so that you keep your back truck in the air. As you approach the end of the curb, give your board a little push to clear your back trucks and extend your back leg so that your board levels off to land.

Backside nosegrind

Practice K grind

K grind

Approach the curb at a slight angle so you can ollie straight into the krooked grind. Place your front foot a bit higher than usual and angle it slightly. Ollie about a foot and a half away from the curb. As you reach the

height of your ollie, push the nose down so the front truck and nose rest on the curb. The front truck and nose of the board are secured in the grind position by putting all your weight on your front foot. Your back foot rests lightly on the back of the board and your

shoulders should be at the same angle as the board. This trick is easier to learn on a curb with an end you can grind off of.

Frontside 180 nosegrind

Ride parallel to the curb with your feet in the ollie
position at a distance a little over a foot. Do a frontside
180 ollie and turn your shoulders. When you have
almost completed your 180, extend your front foot so

that your front truck lands in the grind position. All your weight should be on your front leg to stay in the grind position. Grind off the curb and ride away fakie.

Frontside 180 nosegrind

Backside 180 nosegrind

Approach the curb with your feet in the ollie position.
Do a backside 180 ollie about a foot from the curb.
Start turning your shoulders before the ollie. Just before
you complete the backside 180, extend your front leg

so that you land with your front truck on the curb. Be careful not to lean too far forward or you will slip out. Hold the grind off the curb and ride away fakie.

Backside 180 nosegrind

11

Pop shuvit nosegrind

Before doing this trick you must master the pop shuvit. This is a pop with your back foot so that the board does a 180 underneath your feet. Your back foot does an ollie, and as you ollie, push your foot backward so

that the board spins. A slight push will spin it 180.

For pop shuvit nosegrinds, you approach the curb at a slight angle. Pop shuvit the board about a foot from the curb and place your foot on the nose as it comes

around. Extend your front foot so that it lands in the nosegrind position. Your back foot should be resting lightly on the tail over the trucks. If you are having trouble with this trick, you should practice doing pop shuvits up the curb landing with the nose pressed down.

Switch nosegrind

Any skateboard trick can be done switch stance. Switch is opposite the way you would normally stand. When you first learn tricks, switch will be very uncomfortable and frustrating. Apply the same technique switch as in

your regular stance. Approach the curb riding switch with your front facing the curb. Begin to ollie when you are about six inches from the curb. When you level off in the air, extend your front leg so the nose points down. The front truck should land on the curb.

9 **10**

11

Keep your front leg extended and your back leg slightly bent to hold the grind. As you begin to come off the curb, give the board a little push forward with your front foot so your back truck doesn't hit the curb. After you give the board the push, extend your back leg to level out so you land on both sets of wheels.

Switch krooked grind

While riding switch, approach the curb at a slight angle so you ollie straight into the krooked grind. Your front foot should be a bit higher than usual and slightly angled. Ollie about a foot and a half away from the

curb. As you reach the height of your ollie, push the nose down so that your front truck and nose rest on the curb. The front truck and nose of the board should be secured in the grind position by having all your weight on your front foot. Your back foot should rest

lightly on the back of the board and your shoulders should be angled the same as the board. This trick is easier to learn on a curb that has an ending you can grind off of.

Nollie K grind

Approach the curb at the same angle as a K grind. Your feet should be in nollie position with your front foot on the nose and your back foot in the middle of the board. Pop a nollie about foot and a half from the curb.

While in the air, extend your front foot so that your weight holds the board in the K grind position. Many individuals lean too far over their front truck and come to a complete stop. In order to grind and stay in control, it is necessary to lean back slightly.

When you approach the end of the curb, give your board a push so you miss the end of the curb with your back wheels.

Frontside noseslide

Approach the curb with your front facing the curb. Begin the trick about a foot and a half away from the curb so you land with your nose on the curb. As you ollie, turn your shoulders 90 degrees and slide your

front foot up the board. Land with your weight on the nose with the front wheels pressing into the curb. The front wheels and nose make your board slide. As you slide keep looking forward.

When you reach the end of your slide, turn your shoulders and lower body. Turning off the curb will complete the slide.

11   **12**

13

Backside noseslide

Approach the curb with your back toward it. Begin
your ollie approximately a foot and a half away from
the curb. As you begin to ollie, turn your shoulders so
you land with the nose resting on the curb.

Your approach to the curb should be almost parallel to it or at a slight angle. As the nose lands on the curb, make sure the front wheels are pressed tightly against the curb to ensure that you slide.

When you begin to slow down on your slide, turn your shoulders back to being parallel with the curb and your legs will follow.

Kickflip noseslide

Approach the curb with your feet in a frontside flip
position (your front foot is on the edge of the board
and at a 45 degree angle). You should be about a foot
and a half away from the curb when you begin the

kickflip. Do a 90-degree ollie as if you were doing a
noseslide and combine it with a flip. Most people find
it easier if they pretend they are doing a frontside flip
in order to get the board to do the 90-degree turn with
the flip. Have the nose flipping over the curb so when

the board is done flipping, you can push your foot down and land on the edge of the curb in the nose-slide position.

Frontside tailslide

Approach the curb at a slight angle. Ollie up, turning your shoulders as if you were going to do a frontside 180. Stop when your shoulders arrive at a 90-degree angle to the curb. During your slide, move your weight

to your back foot and keep the wheels pressed into the curb. If you want to come out regular, begin turning your front foot into the curb. Your wheels will stop sliding and you should land riding forward. If you want to come out fakie, lean back slightly and bring your

front foot back and your back foot forward so that you land riding backward.

Backside tailslide

Approach the curb at a slight angle and think about
doing a backside 180. The object is to ollie and begin
turning 180 so the tail lands on the curb. Land with
your weight on your back foot. In order to slide, you

need your weight on the tail and both back wheels tight against the curb. Look forward as you slide. Turn your shoulders and legs so that you ride away regular.

If you want to ride away fakie, you must turn your front foot and your back foot slightly as you slide off the curb.

Kickflip backside tailslide

Master the kickflip and backside kickflip before you try this trick. As you approach the curb, prepare to do a backside tailslide but keep your front foot in a kickflip position. Instead of a backside 180, do a backside kick-

flip. To land this trick, you need to practice letting the board spin under your feet and slamming your feet down with your weight on your back foot and the board in the tailslide position. After the slide turn out regular or fakie.

Practice blunt

Frontside bluntslide

Approach the curb at a slight angle with your back facing the curb and your feet in the ollie position. You should be about a foot from the curb when you begin your ollie. Keep your board angled upward through the

ollie. When you land press the tail against the curb with your back foot and position the top of your wheels on top of the curb. Lean your shoulders back slightly and face forward.

At the end of the curb, turn your leading shoulder forward and square your shoulders parallel to the curb.

Backside bluntslide

Approach the curb at a slight angle with your feet in the ollie position. As you ollie keep your board angled upward and push the tail into the curb so that you are in the blunt position. Keep your weight centered so

you don't slip out. This trick slides easier than the frontside bluntslide. At the end of the curb, turn your shoulders and legs so that you are riding forward.

Backside bluntslide

Backside noseblunt slide

Many skateboarders find this trick rather difficult. The easiest way to learn it is on a box or curb that you can approach head on. As you approach, begin a backside 180 and during the turn extend your front leg so that

the nose turns down. Push it down with your front foot so you land in the noseblunt position (front wheels are on top of the curb and your nose is on the edge). Look forward as you slide. At the end of the curb, turn your shoulders so they are facing forward.

Then extend your back leg as you come off so you land with all four wheels on the ground.

Frontside noseblunt slide

Approach the curb at an angle and do a frontside 180 ollie. In the air extend your front leg so that your nose is pointing down. Land so your front wheels are resting on top of the curb and your nose is resting on the edge

of the curb. All your weight should be on your front leg. At the end of the curb, turn your shoulders forward or backward depending on whether you want to ride away regular or fakie.

Noseblunt slides are done with your front wheels. The nose simply holds the slide in position.

Half cab noseblunt slide

Learn this trick on a box as shown to help make it a lot easier. Ride up to the ledge fakie and do a half cab ollie that clears the box. When you get above the curb, bring your feet around so that you are able to slide parallel

along the curb. The secret to this trick is putting pressure on the nose. Your weight should be predominantly on your front foot. Your back foot should just hold the board in place.

At the end of the curb bring your feet around so you come off facing forward.

Nollie frontside noseslide

Approach the curb at a slight angle with your feet in the nollie position (your front foot on the nose and your back foot in the middle of the board). Begin the nollie about a foot away from the curb.

Give the nose a snap against the ground for the nollie, and while you are in the air, turn the board so it lands in the noseslide position. Keep the nose against the curb and have your weight over your front foot to hold the board in position.

At the end of the curb, turn your shoulders back so you can turn out regular.

Half cab noseslide

Approach the curb riding fakie (backward) to about a foot and a half from the curb. Keep looking forward. Pop your tail like you were doing a fakie ollie. Turn your front foot in the air so that your board and feet

make a 90-degree turn. During the turn in the air, move your front foot up on the board so that the nose lands on the curb. Put most of your weight on the front foot so the board is held in the noseslide position. As you come to the end of your slide, turn your shoulders to

complete the 180-degree turn so you are riding forward.

Nollie tailslide

Approach the curb as you would for a half cab nose-slide but ride forward. Start the trick approximately a foot and a half away from the curb. Place your front foot on the nose and your back foot in the middle of

the board. Pop a nollie 180, and while turning 180, extend your back foot so that when your tail is over the curb it lands in the tailslide position. Shift your weight to your back leg to stay in the tailslide position.

Once you have slowed down on your slide, turn your front foot either forward or backward in order to come out regular or fakie.

Nollie 5-0

Approach the curb with your front foot on the nose
and your back foot in the middle of the board. Ride
parallel to the curb at a distance of about six inches.
Pop a nollie and when your board reaches maximum

height, extend your back foot so that you land 5-0. Your weight should be on the back foot in order to hold your grind. When you grind off, extend your front foot slightly so your board lands level on the ground.

Nollie nosegrind

Ride parallel to the curb at a distance of about six inches. Your feet should be in the nollie position with your front foot on the nose and your back foot in the middle of the board. Pop your nollie and as the board

reaches maximum height, slightly push your front foot out and extend it so that you land in the nosegrind position. This push with your foot gives the board the momentum needed to land in the nosegrind position.

As you near the end of the curb, give your feet a quick push forward so the back trucks clear the curb.

Frontside smith grind

This trick requires your weight to be on your back foot
to hold the board in grind position while your front
foot simply holds the front of the board below the
curb. Ollie about a foot and a half from the curb as in a

50-50 grind, but land your front truck off the curb.
Land your back truck and keep all of your weight centered over it. Your front foot simply rests on the board
and keeps it pointed below the curb. This trick is best
learned on a curb that has an ending point. As you

approach the end of the curb, push on the tail in order to bring the nose up to the same level as the back truck. When your board levels out prepare to land and ride away.

Backside smith grind

Like the frontside smith grind, this trick requires all
your weight to be on the back truck to hold it in the
grind position. Approach the curb at a 40-degree angle
and ollie up so that you land with your back truck

slammed against the curb. To get the best locked position, get your outside wheel as close to the curb as possible. As you lock in your back truck, your front truck should be off the curb. Point the nose down with your front foot. At the end of the curb, lift up on the tail so

the nose comes up and levels out the board. When your board levels in the air prepare to land and ride away.

Frontside lipslide

Approach the curb at about a 40-degree angle with your front facing the curb. Your feet should be in ollie position. When your nose is about six inches from the curb, do a frontside 180 so that your back wheels are

162

over the curb and your front wheels are hanging off
the edge. Your back wheels and board produce the
slide for this trick. Make sure the curb is well waxed.

At the end of your slide, push the board forward and turn your front foot and back foot so that your board is parallel to the curb. The pushing and turning cause you to come off the curb.

Backside lipslide

Approach the curb backward at a 40-degree angle. Do a backside 180 about six inches from the curb. As you turn backside, keep your shoulders facing forward in order to keep your balance while sliding. When your

board 180s over the curb, land your back wheels on top of the curb with your front wheels hanging off. Continue to keep your shoulders facing forward and your knees bent to aid in the sliding process. When you are near the end of your slide, push your board forward

and rotate your feet so that you are parallel to the curb. This pushing and rotating will help you come off the ledge. If you are doing the trick on a curb with an end, rotate your feet so that you land riding forward.

Fakie ollie switch 5-0 grind

Keep about a foot distance in your backward approach and look over your back shoulder. Pop a fakie ollie, and while in the air, extend your front leg so that your board lands in the 5-0 position.

At the end of the curb you should be able to grind off and ride away fakie.

Fakie ollie switch 5-0 grind

Fakie ollie tailslide

Ride fakie and approach at a 40-degree angle with your
back to the curb. Your back foot should be on the tail
and your front foot in the middle of the board. When
your nose is about six inches from the curb, pop a

fakie ollie. Ollie up so that your tail clears the curb and bring it backward so that the board locks into a tail-slide. When you are nearing the end of your slide, turn your body and feet either left or right so that you come out fakie or regular.

Fakie ollie tailslide

11

Fakie ollie frontside tailslide

Approach at a 40-degree angle riding fakie with your
front facing the curb. Your back foot should be on the
tail and your front foot in the middle of the board.
When your nose is about six inches from the curb,

pop a fakie ollie. Ollie up so that your tail clears the curb and bring it backward so the board locks into a tailslide. To help keep your balance look over your front shoulder like you would in a frontside boardslide.

When you are nearing the end of your slide, turn your body and feet either left or right so that you come out fakie or regular.

Resources

For a quick fix go to **www.skateboarding.com** — an informative (but not the only) portal into the skateboarding galaxy.

Books
Discovered on **amazon.com** and **barnesandnoble.com**.

Baccigaluppi, John. *Declaration of Independents*. San Francisco, California: Chronicle Books, 2001.

Bermudez, Ben. *Skate! The Mongo's Guide to Skateboarding*. New York, New York: Cheapskate Press, 2001.

Borden, Ian. *Skateboarding, Space and the City*. New York, New York: Berg, 2001.

Brooke, Michael. *The Concrete Wave: The History of Skateboarding*. Toronto, Ontario: Warwick Publishing, 1999.

Burke, L.M. *Skateboarding! Surf the Pavement*. New York, New York: Rosen Publishing Group, Inc., 1999.

Davis, James. *Skateboard Roadmap*. England: Carlton Books Limited, 1999.

Gould, Marilyn. *Skateboarding*. Mankato, Minnesota: Capstone Press, 1991.

Gutman, Bill. *Skateboarding: To the Extreme*. New York, New York: Tom Doherty Associates, Inc., 1997.

Hawk, Tony. *Hawk*. New York, New York: Regan Books, 2001.

Powell, Ben. *Extreme Sports: Skateboarding*. Hauppauge, New York: Barron's Educational Series, Inc., 1999.

Riggins, Edward. *Ramp Plans*. San Francisco, California: High Speed Productions, 2000.

Ryan, Pat. *Extreme Skateboarding*. Mankato, Minnesota: Capstone Press, 1998.

Shoemaker, Joel. *Skateboarding Streetstyle*. Mankato, Minnesota: Capstone Press, 1995.

Thrasher. *Insane Terrain*. New York, New York: Universe Publishing, 2001.

Camps
Donny Barley Skate Camp
1747 West Main Road
Middletown, Rhode Island
02842
401-848-8078

Lake Owen
HC 60 Box 60
Cable, Wisconsin 54821
715-798-3785

Magdalena Ecke Family YMCA
200 Saxony Road
Encinitas, California 92023-0907
760-942-9622

Mission Valley YMCA
5505 Friars Road
San Diego, California 92110
619-298-3576

Skatelab
Steve Badillo Skate Camp
4226 Valley Fair Street
Simi Valley, California 93063
805-578-0040
vtaskate@aol.com

Snow Valley
PO Box 2337
Running Springs, California
92382
909-867-2751

Visalia YMCA
Sequoia Lake, California
211 West Tulare Avenue
Visalia, California 93277
559-627-0700

Woodward Camp
Box 93
Route 45
Woodward, Pennsylvania 16882
814-349-5633

Young Life Skate Camp
Hope, British Columbia, Canada
604-807-3718

Magazines
Big Brother
www.bigbrothermagazine.com

Skateboarder
Surfer Publications
PO Box 1028
Dana Point, California 92629

Thrasher
High Speed Productions
1303 Underwood Avenue
San Francisco, California 94124
415-822-3083
www.thrashermagazine.com

Transworld Skateboarding
353 Airport Road
Oceanside, California 92054
760-722-7777
www.skateboarding.com

Museums
Huntington Beach International
Skate and Surf Museum
411 Olive Street
Huntington Beach, California
714-960-3483

Skatelab
4226 Valley Fair
Simi Valley, California
805-578-0040
www.skatelab.com

Skatopia
34961 Hutton Road
Rutland, Ohio 45775
740-742-1110

Organizations, movers, shakers . . .
Action Sports Retailer
Organizer of the Action Sports
Retailer Trade Expos
949-376-8144
www.asrbiz.com

California Amateur Skateboard
League (CASL) and PSL
Amateur and professional
contest organizer
909-883-6176
Fax 909-883-8036

The Canadian Cup
416-960-2222

Extreme Downhill International
1666 Garnet Avenue #308
San Diego, California 92109
619-272-3095

International Association of
Skateboard Companies (IASC)
PO Box 37
Santa Barbara, California 93116
805-683-5676
Fax 805-967-7537
iascsk8@aol.com
www.skateboardiasc.org

International Network
for Flatland Freestyle
Skateboarding
Abbedissavagen 15
746 95 Balsta, Sweden

KC Projects
Canadian amateur contest
organizer
514-806-7838
kc_projects@aol.com
5148067838@fido.ca

National Amateur Skateboard
Championships
Damn Am Series
National amateur contest
organizer
813-621-6793
www.skateparkoftampa.com
www.nascseries.com

National Skateboarders
Association of Australia (NSAA)
Amateur and professional
contest organizers
61-2-9878-3876
www.skateboard.asn.au

The Next Cup
Southern California amateur
contest organizer
858-874-4970 ext. 114 or 129
www.thenextcup.com

Real Amateur Skateboarding
Amateur contest organizer
619-501-1341
realamateurskateboarding
@hotmail.com

Skateboarding Association of
America
Amateur contest organizer
727-523-0875
www.skateboardassn.org

Skatepark Association of the
USA (SPAUSA)
Resource for skatepark
planning/operating
310-823-9228
www.spausa.org

Southwest Sizzler
Southwestern amateur contest
organizer
918-638-6492

Surf Expo
East Coast trade show
800-947-SURF
www.surfexpo.com

United Skateboarding
Association (USA)
Skate event organizer
and action sport marketing/
promotions
732-432-5400
ext. 2168 and 2169
www.unitedskate.com

Vans Shoes
Organizer of the Triple Crown
skate events
562-565-8267
www.vans.com

World Cup Skateboarding
Organizer of some of skating's
largest events
530-888-0596
Fax 530-888-0296
danielle@wcsk8.com
www.wcsk8.com

Zeal Skateboarding Association
Southern California amateur
contest organizer
909-265-3420
www.zealsk8.com

**Public skateparks /
information about building
and starting up**

Consolidated Skateboards
(see *The Plan*)
www.consolidatedskateboard
.com

International Association of
Skateboard Companies (IASC)
PO Box 37
Santa Barbara, California 93116
805-683-5676
Fax 805-967-7537
iascsk8@aol.com
www.skateboardiasc.org

Skatepark Association of the
USA (SPAUSA)
310-823-9228
www.spausa.org

www.skatepark.org

**Public skatepark designers /
builders**
Airspeed Skateparks LLC
2006 Highway 101 #154
Florence, Oregon 97439
503-791-4674
airspeed@airspeedskateparks
.com
www.airspeedskateparks.com

CA Skateparks, Design/Build
and General Contracting
273 North Benson Avenue
Upland, California 91786
562-208-4646
www.skatedesign.com

Dreamland Skateparks,
Grindline, Inc.
4056 23rd Avenue SW
Seattle, Washington 98106
206-933-7915
www.grindline.com

Ramptech
www.ramptech.com

SITE Design Group, Inc.
414 South Mill Avenue,
Suite 210
Tempe, Arizona 85281
480-894-6797
Fax 480-894-6792
mm@sitedesigngroup.com
www.sitedesigngroup.com

Spectrum Skatepark
Creations, Ltd.
M/A 2856 Clifftop Lane
Whistler, B.C.
V0N 1B2 Canada
250-238-0140
design@spectrum-sk8.com
www.spectrum-sk8.com

Team Pain
864 Gazelle Trail
Winter Springs, Florida 32708
407-695-8215
tim@teampain.com
www.teampain.com

John Woodstock Designs
561-743-5963
johnwoodstock@msn.com
www.woodstockskateparks.com

**Shops / skateparks
finding one close to you**
Two (among quite a few) that
will help:
www.skateboarding.com
www.skateboards.org

**Television
ESPN**
X Games
espn.go.com/extreme

NBC
Gravity Games
www.gravitygames.com

Web sites
www.board-trac.com
Market researchers for skateboarding industry.

www.bigbrother.com
A comprehensive site by *Big
Brother* magazine.

www.exploratorium.edu/
skateboarding
Glossary, scientific explanations
and equipment for skating.

www.interlog.com/~mbrooke/
skategeezer.html
International Longboarder
magazine.

www.ncdsa.com
Northern California Downhill
Skateboarding Association.

www.skateboardiasc.org
International Association of
Skateboard Companies (IASC) is
one of the leading advocates of
skateboarding progress and pro-
vides a wealth of information.

www.skateboard.com
Chat and messages.

www.skateboarding.com
Every skater's site by
Transworld Skateboarding
magazine.

www.skateboards.org
Find parks, shops and companies.

www.skatelab.com
One of Los Angeles area's
largest indoor parks and world's
largest skateboard museum.

www.skater.net
Skate parks and ramp plans.

www.smithgrind.com
Skate news wire.

www.switchmagazine.com
*Switch Skateboarding
Magazine.*

www.thrashermagazine.com
A comprehensive site by
Thrasher magazine.

Videos / Instructional

411 Video Productions. *The
First Step.*

411 Video Productions. *The
Next Step.*

Hawk, Tony. *Tony Hawk's Trick
Tips Volume I: Skateboarding
Basics.* 900 Films, 2001.

Hawk, Tony. *Tony Hawk's Trick
Tips Volume II: Essentials of
Street.* 900 Films, 2001.

Thrasher Magazine. *How to
Skateboard.* San Francisco,
California: High Speed
Productions, Inc., 1995.

Thrasher Magazine. *How to
Skateboard Better.* San
Francisco, California: High
Speed Productions, Inc., 1997.

Transworld Skateboarding.
Starting Point. Oceanside,
California, 1997.

Transworld Skateboarding. *Trick
Tips with Wily Santos.*
Oceanside, California, 1998.

Transworld Skateboarding.
Starting Point Number Two.
Oceanside, California, 1999.

Index